BMH-79128

Locks and Keys

COLLECTORS' BLUE BOOKS

Locks and Keys

LOUIS ZARA

WALKER AND COMPANY, NEW YORK

Page 1: Persian combination padlock with calligraphic inscriptions. Four inner barrels rotate for combination. Bronze. Safavid period, 17th century. 4¾ in. Walters Art Gallery, Baltimore.

Frontispiece: African lock from Mali, made by the Bambara. Wood and brass. 18 in. high. The Museum of Primitive Art, New York.

Library of Congress Catalog Card Number: 79-86410

First published in the United States of America in 1969 by the Walker Publishing Company, Inc.

Published simultaneously in Canada by The Ryerson Press, Toronto

Printed in the United States of America
Jacket design by the Bert Clarke Design Group
Book design by Joseph Bourke Del Valle

ACKNOWLEDGMENTS

I AM HEAVILY INDEBTED to the remarkable John M. Mossman Collection of Locks and Keys, now housed at the Mechanics' Institute of New York, and to Robert E. Hoffman, secretary and treasurer of the General Society of Mechanics and Tradesmen of the City of New York, who provided photographs and extended to me many thoughtful courtesies while I studied the collection.

I am also indebted to the Schlage Lock Company of San Francisco, which granted me permission for the use of photographs of locks and keys in their famous Antique Lock Collection. And, of course, it would have been difficult to proceed without the many courtesies offered by the management of Eaton, Yale & Towne, Inc. relating to the use of negatives of all the items in the historic Yale & Towne Lock Collection.

I acknowledge also the splendid cooperation of the Lips Safe and Lock Company of Dordrecht, Holland, which supplied me with many important photographs from their great collection. In particular am I indebted to *Locks and Keys Throughout the Ages* by the late Vincent J. M. Eras, managing director of the Lips organization and, incidentally, founder of their collection at the inspiration of the above-mentioned John M. Mossman.

I also gratefully acknowledge permissions and attendant courtesies from the following: Bavarian National Museum, Munich; The British Museum, London; City Art Museum of St. Louis; Cooper-Hewitt Museum of Design, New York; Field Museum of Natural History, Chicago; German National Museum, Nürnberg; Hispanic Society of New York; Mercer Museum, Bucks County Historical Society, Doylestown, Pennsylvania; The Metropolitan Museum of Art, New York; Musée de Cluny, Paris; Musée et Institut d'Ethnographie, Geneva; Musée le Secq des Tournelles, Rouen; Museo Nazionale (Bargello), Florence; Museum of Fine Arts, Boston; Museum of Primitive Art, New York; Museum Princessehof, Leeuwarden; Museum Vleeshuis and the Board of Burgomaster and Aldermen, City of Antwerp; Pennsylvania Farm Museum of Landis Valley, Lancaster; Philadelphia Museum of Art; Rijks Museum, Amsterdam; University College, London; Victoria and Albert Museum, London; The Wallace Collection, London; Walters Art Gallery, Baltimore.

I am indebted to Frank Caro of New York for photographing his Imperial K'ang Hsi bronze padlock for this volume. For leads on Egyptian locks, I thank Bernard V. Bothmer, Curator of Ancient Art, The Brooklyn Museum. For information on early American locks, I wish to acknowledge Henry J. Kauffman of Lancaster, Pennsylvania. For unfailing courtesy over the long period this study was in progress, I thank Mary A. Danforth of the Schlage Lock Company. And for keen editorial vigilance, I pay warm tribute to my very able editor Joan Vass.

Above: Spanish lock plate with three pairs of facing animals, for Varqueño chest. Brass. 17th century. The Hispanic Society of America, New York.

Opposite: Unusual Roman key with bust of youth. Bronze. 1st or 2nd century. Lips Collection, Dordrecht.

Above left: French marriage coffret key, for Savoy-Visconti wedding. Carved steel. Ca. 1520. 4¾ in. Center: American colonial folding key from Philadelphia mansion. Steel. Ca. 1785. Open: 5½ in. Right: French armoire key with ace of clubs form in shank and barrel plug, or "pipe." Steel. 18th century. Key: 6 in.; plug: 1⅜ in. Author's collection.

Below: Roman ring key. Bronze. Lips Collection, Dordrecht.

GLOSSARY

Barrel key: a key that has a hollow shank.

Bit: the blade that projects from the shank and contains the steps or notches and indentations; that part of the key inserted first into the keyhole.

Bolt: the piece that slides out of the lock case and fits into the socket or receptacle on the doorframe, thus closing the lock.

Bow: that part grasped by the fingers when the key is inserted into the lock; in early keys often elaborated with finials and designs.

Combination lock: a lock that is opened by setting a dial or dials to a previously agreed combination of numbers or letters.

Cylinder: the short cylindrical plug that contains the keyhole and the pin-tumbler mechanism which is worked by the key.

Dead bolt: the square or round bolt which is moved in or out by the key.

Double-throw lock: a lock having a bolt which, after the first turn of the key that brings it out, can be brought out still farther by additional turns of the key; of course, it takes an equal full turn to bring it back.

Latch: a lock with a beveled spring bolt which acts by itself when a door is closed.

Night latch: a spring-bolt lock that is operated by a key from the outside and by a knob from the inside.

Padlock: a lock that is not permanently inserted or affixed but hangs via a shackle from a hasp and staple.

Pin key: a key that has a solid shank.

Shank: the central part of the key between the bow and the bit.

Stem: shank.

Skeleton key: key whose bit is cut away to avoid the obstructions inside the lock and still lift the tumbler and move the bolt.

Ward: a fixed projection in a lock that will keep a key from entering or turning unless the key has notches that will fit it.

Stump: a circular pin within the case of the lock which guides different working parts. In lever locks the stump works in a slot in the lever called a gating.

Tumbler: a unit in the mechanism that holds or releases the bolt. The right key lifts it and "shoots" the bolt.

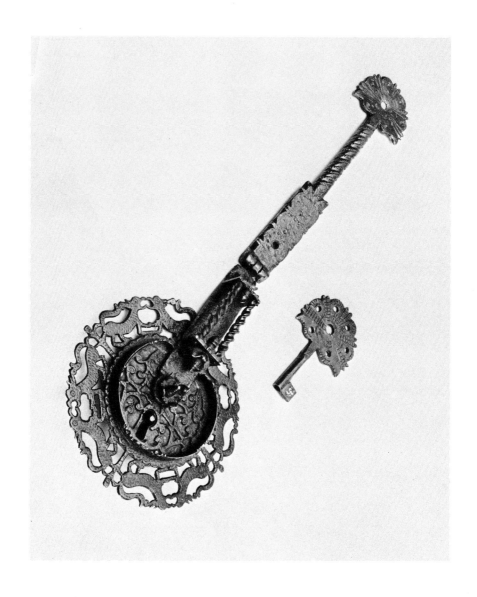

Spanish lock and key from coffer of Queen Isabella, with hinged hasp, rim or lock plate pierced with pairs of facing animals. Wrought iron. Ca. 1474–1504. Schlage Antique Lock Collection, San Francisco.

"Lock-and-key, *n.* The distinguishing device of civilization and enlightenment."   —*The Devil's Dictionary,* Ambrose Bierce

THE BEST COLLECTIONS of locks and keys are in England, France, Holland and the United States, but there are splendid holdings in Germany and in Italy, as well as fine private collections everywhere.

Yet, except for meager catalog descriptions, little has been written on locks or keys in any language. All the more surprising, then, that museums and dealers bid eagerly for every interesting specimen that reaches the market, and today more and more individual collectors are looking for them.

Few objects are so familiar, but somehow the air of secrecy that, since antiquity, has attended the construction of locks and keys follows them even when they are collected. A man may boast of his rare coins, watches, clocks or porcelains; he is not so likely to broadcast that he collects locks and keys—as if such could only be an accumulation of odd hardware.

The lack of wide public recognition has been unfortunate—except to those collectors who therefore have been able to buy fine locks and keys at very modest prices. The neglect has resulted in a gap in the overall history of craftsmanship. From a study of the role played by the lock and key in society, a whole treatise might be written on the development of the sense of property and the increased value placed on individual privacy—to say nothing of the ingenuity of the mechanisms and the artistry of the designs.

Various circumstances may be responsible for this omission. For example, early American ironwork has been praised and collected, but the handcrafting of locks and keys in the American colonies has been ignored on the assumption that the early locks and keys were always imported from the mother country. For the same reason, early locks and keys in Canada and in Latin America also have been neglected.

Considerations of security may have been a factor. Not only has little been written about the cultural and esthetic aspects of locks and keys, still less has been written about the construction of them—about locksmithing itself.

While nearly every book on ironwork, for example, includes a few illustrations of ornate locks and handsome keys from Gothic and Renaissance times, the pictures are seldom accompanied by explanations worth reading. As if the guild of master locksmiths had decreed that forevermore no one should give away its secrets!

There always have been reasons to be discreet. Since the essential purpose of the lock is security, it might be argued that explication of its mechanics would undermine the whole system of safety that the lock and the key promise to maintain. Nevertheless, it is right to question whether that argument is valid, for most of those who pick locks learn their tricks not from books but from locksmithing or from working in lock-manufacturing plants. Besides, anyone who is handy with tools and enjoys tinkering can master the principles of the lock without going to the library.

What is offered in the pages that follow is given in the conviction that all men have the right to learn anything they can absorb. Indeed, the lack of straightforward information has given the public a false sense of security in just ordinary locking devices. If more people understood how easily poorly made locks can be opened by amateurs, there would be a greater demand for the fine modern locks that are as close to being pickproof as mechanical ingenuity can make them.

At its best, the lock is ingenious, and the key, so guileless in appearance, is an extraordinary device. Together or separately, they are part of man's cultural history and deserve as much attention as the wheel, the clock, the steam engine, the camera, the internal combustion motor, or any other invention. They reflect the tastes of the periods in which they were created, and the finer examples are to be appreciated as superb, though minor, objets d'art.

Locks and Keys pays homage to the fertile imaginations that created them, to the esthetic sensibilities of the anonymous craftsmen who embellished them, and to the splendid inventors and engineers who have sought to improve them for the greater privacy and security of all.

Bronze African keys from Benin. 19th century or earlier. Upper left: bow with human heads and rope elements. 5⅛ in. Lower left: 5⅛ in. Right: possibly a royal key. Bow with human and leopard heads over collar simulating coral beads. Overall: 15⅛ in.; key: 7⅜ in. Field Museum of Natural History, Chicago.

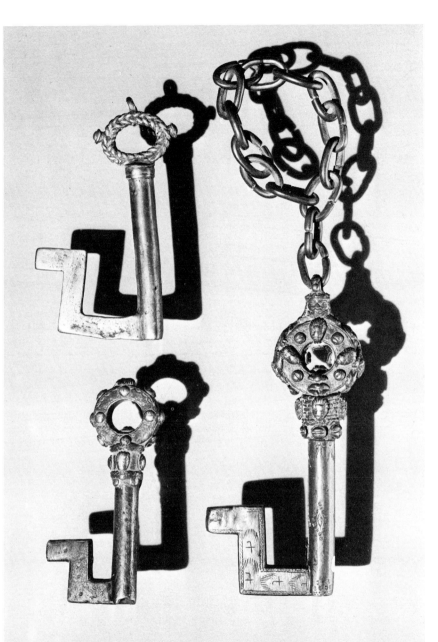

Egyptian key for sarcophagus of Ptolemy II Philadelphus. Bronze 283–246 B.C.
Lips Collection, Dordrecht.

CHAPTER I

What Is a Lock? What Is a Key?

"Open locks, whoever knocks."—*Macbeth*

LE CORBUSIER, THE ARCHITECT, called the building "a machine for living in." The lock could be called "a machine for keeping in and keeping out." For a lock is a fastening, a device to hold fast a door, a gate, or a drawer to which it may be affixed, and to keep it from being opened. Primarily, the lock consists of a bolt, or a substitute for a bolt, that can be caused to remain in a definite fixed position until an "authorized implement" releases it. That authorized implement is the key. In the modern, complicated lock mechanisms that protect safes and bank vaults the release may be effected by special arrangements, or combinations, of numbers, letters, or mechanical or electrical devices.

There are many kinds of locks; here we will explain and illustrate the most important types from earliest antiquity to those in general use today. We will be concerned with keys and with the locks that keys operate, although we may occasionally glance at keyless and combination devices. The key, attractive for historical or art reasons, is an interesting device even when it is quite ordinary. It can be regarded as an object independent of the lock, although it is easier to appreciate if one understands how it operates within the lock.

The mechanism of the lock contains three main parts: the bolt, the key and an obstacle which the proper key must avoid or thrust aside before it can operate the bolt. The bolt works in and out. Normally, it slides, but it can be made to pivot or to rotate. The key usually turns or rotates, but it can, as in the Chinese padlock, work by sliding or pushing. Obstacles can be of various kinds. In the lock that has wards, which are projections inside around the keyhole, cuts or steps in the bit of the key that correspond to the wards will bypass the projecting obstacles. In the lock that has tumblers, the cuts or steps in the bit of the key must be made precisely to lift the tumblers. Only when the tumblers are lifted can the bolt be moved.

These statements cover all the basic operations of the lock mechanism.

The key may be considered as having four parts. The end that is grasped in the fingers is the bow. The midsection, which is the narrowest part, is the shank. The end that is inserted into the lock, or into the keyhole, is the bit. The variations in the bit, which may be in graduated cuts, steps, inlets or slots, are called the steps.

The relationship between lock and key has been stated clearly by Vincent J. M. Eras: "The design of the key predetermines the design of the lock mechanism, which means that the key is made first and the lock afterwards. Subsequently, the key bit constitutes the principal part of the key, since this part brings about the locking and unlocking of the mechanism."

Remembering these facts and the definitions of the basic terms will make it easier to understand any exposition about locks and keys.

Above: American combination padlock. Brass, except for iron shackle. Mid-19th century. 2¾ in. long. John M. Mossman Collection of Locks and Keys, New York.

COLOR PLATE 1 Top: English Bramah lock. Steel. Early 19th century. Bottom: Russian chain of miniature padlocks, made for Catherine II (1762–1796). Platinum. Schlage Antique Lock Collection, San Francisco.

CHAPTER II

Facts and Superstitions

"All the keys hang not at one man's girdle."   —Old proverb
"They say he wears a key in his ear and a lock hanging by it."
—Much Ado About Nothing

THOUGH KEYS WERE NOT BESTOWED upon man on the day of his creation, they were conceived and became part of his folklore early in recorded history. Both his religion and his mythology attest to their place in his thinking.

In Babylon, the god Marduk was said to have made both the gates and the keys to Heaven. Ishtar the goddess must have possessed a full set of keys, for she could open the seven gates and locks of Hell. According to the Greeks, the goddess Athena carried the keys of her city Athens, while Hecate carried the keys of the universe, and Hades had iron bars and keys. According to the Romans, the two-faced god Janus carried keys in both hands. The goddesses Ceres and Cybele both were adorned with keys, and the god Mithra, too, had a key. In Rome, a new bride was given keys at her wedding, but when she was divorced she had to surrender them. In Alexandria, it was Serapis who held the keys to the land and the sea.

In Matthew, Jesus said to Peter: "I will give unto thee the keys of the kingdom of Heaven." (Those are the keys on the coat of arms of the Holy See.) In the Book of Revelation, the key of the bottomless pit was in the hand of an angel.

In Germany, the key was an amulet against the Evil Eye. In Italy, tiny keys prevented convulsions in infants. In Gaul, a widow laid her keys upon the corpse of her husband. In China, an only son was given a key to lock him fast into life and living; among the well-to-do the key might be a flat plaque of jade carved in the outline of a Chinese padlock and hung about the child's neck.

In the year 600, Pope Gregory the Great sent Childebert, the king of the Franks, a golden key to wear around his neck to guard him from evil.

Abyssinian steel key. Date uncertain. The Wallace Collection, London.

In Russia, a key was held in the hand to stop bleeding. In Scotland and in Staffordshire in England, a key laid on the neck or put down the back stopped bleeding at the nose. In the seventeenth century in Scotland, secrets were brought to light by the turning of a key. A century later, a Scottish woman was accused of laying a key under a sick man's pillow to cure him, presumably by witchcraft. Among the Bengal Hindus, mourners wore iron or iron keys.

James G. Frazer, author of *The Golden Bough: A Study in Magic and Religion,* collected numerous superstitions that demonstrated how tenaciously locks and keys had taken hold of folk imagination. He recorded that during the Middle Ages, and down to the eighteenth century, it was commonly held in Europe that the consummation of marriage could be prevented by anyone who, while the wedding ceremony was taking place, either locked a lock or tied a knot with a cord, and then threw the lock or the cord away. The lock or the knotted cord had to be flung into water; until it had been found and unlocked or untied, no real union of the married pair was possible.

No ailing person, man or woman, would dare venture out of his home without a bunch of keys or a knife in his hand for fear that without such a talisman some devil might take advantage of his weak state to slip into his body.

Locks and keys were believed to be particularly efficacious for women in childbirth. On the island of Salsette near Bombay, all locks on doors or drawers were opened with a key to facilitate delivery. In Transylvania, the knots on a woman's garments were untied when she was in travail, and all locks, whether on doors or on chests, were unlocked. In Argyllshire every lock in the house was opened during childbirth.

The act of opening and closing came by extension to embrace not only childbirth but also death. In many parts of England it was thought that a person could not expire as long as any locks were locked or bolts remained thrown in the house. When a sufferer was plainly coming to his last hours it was a common practice to open all locks and bolts so that the final agony should not be prolonged unnecessarily. Shakespeare must have been acquainted with this superstition, for in *Cymbeline* he says, "The sure Physician, Death, who is the key to unbar these locks."

"Key," said Walter Skeat, the great authority on the etymology of the English language, "that which opens or shuts a lock," was formerly pronounced *kay.* The remoter origin of the word is unknown, but it has no connection with "quay," a wharf for vessels, which comes from the Old French and Celtic word for an enclosure. The modern pronunciation of key is from a North British dialect.

Obliquely, key acquired subtle meanings. To be "keyholed" is to be tipsy— perhaps because an inebriated man cannot find the keyhole? "To have the key to the street" is to be shut out for the night, or to have no home. (Dickens used it in *Pickwick Papers*.) "He lay the key under the door" was used as early as the seventeenth century to mean "he went bankrupt."

Not surprisingly, key and lock slipped into vulgar usage, with key standing for the male organ and lock and keyhole for the female. "Key and keyhole sustain like punishment" went an old proverb. Or as Robert Burton in his *Anatomy of Melancholy* said of Jealousy: "If a man have a lock which every man's key will open, as well as his own, why should he think to keep it private to himself?"

Nepal padlock with key inserted at top. Probably 18th century. 15⁹⁄₁₆ in. long. Musée et Institut d'Ethnographie, Geneva.

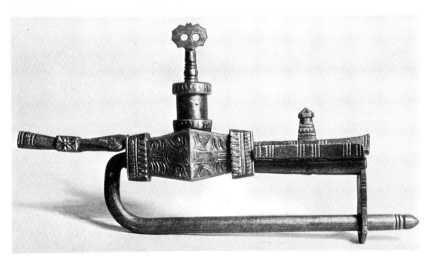

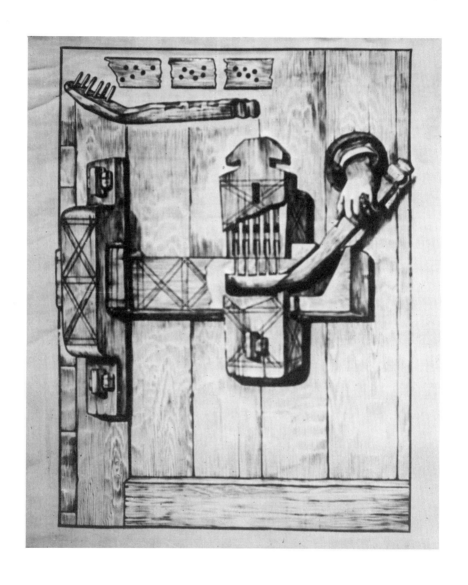

Egyptian lock on door, being opened. Model of key shown above, left. Lips Collection, Dordrecht.

CHAPTER III

Who Invented Lock and Key?

"Pray ye, go: there's my key. If you do stir abroad, go armed."
—*King Lear*

PLINY THE ELDER maintained that the key was invented by Theodorus of Samos in the sixth century B.C. Pliny's curiosity had led him to investigate countless subjects, from butterflies to rubies. In his *Natural History,* which he proudly dedicated to the Emperor Titus, he assembled twenty thousand facts. But on the subject of keys he was dealing with legends. (Incidentally, it was his thirst for facts that goaded him to go ashore for closer observation of Mount Vesuvius in eruption, and so he perished at Stabiae as Pompeii was covered with hot pumice and ashes and Herculaneum was overwhelmed in a sea of lava mud that third week in August, A.D. 79.)

We can only speculate why Pliny attributed the key to Theodorus. Samos was the great center of Ionian civilization in the fifth and sixth centuries B.C. Herodotus called it one of the finest cities of the world. A Theodorus, architect and sculptor, was the son of Rhoecus who invented casting in bronze. Another Theodorus, grandson of the same Rhoecus, was a famous sculptor in bronze and excelled in engraving both metals and gemstones. Pliny singled out the first Theodorus, but either was capable of creating lock mechanisms and their keys for luxury-loving patrons.

However, the actual invention of the lock preceded these Greek artist-craftsmen. Eustathius (a millennium and a half later, to be sure) credited it to the Spartans. He was not consistent either. He also pointed to Book XXI of the *Odyssey,* where Penelope, determined to stay her suitors, was inspired by Athena to put them to trial. Whoever should bend her absent husband's great bow and shoot an arrow through twelve axes should win her. To bring forth that bow, Penelope took "a crooked key in her firm hand—a goodly key of bronze, having an ivory handle." The key was to Ulysses' treasure chamber. "She loosed the strap, thrust in the key, and with a careful aim shot back the door-bolts. As a bull roars when feeding in the field, so roared the goodly door touched by the key, and open flew before her." The language is extravagant

but it is proof enough that locks and keys were available when Homer sang, or wrote, his epics (about 850 B.C.), or three centuries earlier when Troy fell. The model which is shown on page 84 was opened by such "a crooked key" as Penelope used.

The first lock of antiquity of which we have clear physical evidence was found in Persia in 1842 when Paul Emile Botta, the French consul at Mosul, began the digging on the Tigris that launched the era of modern excavation of archeological sites. At Khorsabad, Botta uncovered the ruins of the enormous palace of Sargon II, who reigned 722–705 B.C.; the king called it *Dur Sharrukin,* which means Sargonsburg. There, at the end of a hall, behind tall, winged, man-headed bulls, was a strong single gate that had been closed by a heavy wooden lock. That lock was worked by a key so large that "a full-grown man could hardly carry it alone."

The bar, or bolt, of the lock moved into a square hole in the wall. The key had pegs at the bit end to correspond to as many holes in the wooden bar or bolt. Insert this key so that the pegs rise into the holes. Press down on the handle of the key, and the bolt is engaged. Now it can be lifted, drawn back, and the door can be opened.

According to James H. Breasted, the archeologist, Khorsabad was a mile square and could shelter eighty thousand persons; the residence-palace covered twenty-five acres. In this impressive capital of Assyria were many vaults and arsenals for precious stuffs and weapons. Did the wooden locks provide more protection than the usual armed guards? It pleased King Sargon to have both.

That key, so large and heavy that it took a man to carry it, is the type referred to in Isaiah, xxii, 22: "And the key of the House of David will I lay upon his shoulder; so he shall open, and none shall shut; and he shall shut, and none shall open."

The wooden locks were placed on the *inside* of the door and had no keyholes. Therefore, they could not be opened from the outside by (what we would consider) normal means. Approach the door and you see no keyhole! However, above or adjacent to the place where the lock was affixed inside, a hole had been cut. Through this hole, the owner thrust his hand and key. He

Above: Roman keys. Center shows three keys on circlet for hanging on girdle. Bronze, or iron and bronze. 1st century B.C.–2nd century A.D. Below: Coptic ring key. Bronze. 3rd or 4th century. 3⅜ in. Walters Art Gallery, Baltimore.

inserted the key into the side of the lock and caused the tumbler to lift; then the bolt could be retracted. For such an action, the curved key, as in Homer, or the sickle-shaped key described by other writers, was practical.

To us it seems weird; no keyhole, and a hole in the door. But unless one had the key, the door could not be opened. And if a guard were stationed inside, the groping hand of an intruder would be seized.

A similar lock explains the passage in the Song of Solomon: "I sleep, but my heart waketh: it is the voice of my beloved that knocketh, saying, Open to me, my sister, my love, my dove, my undefiled . . ." followed by: "My beloved put in his hand by the hole of the door. . . ." Evidently, he did not have the key. "I rose up to open to my beloved; and my hands dropped with myrrh, and my fingers with sweet-smelling myrrh upon the handles of the lock."

These references, in the Old Testament and in Homer, tell us that locks and keys were in use in the first millennium B.C. The find from Khorsabad is, of course, impressive, but for the very earliest use of the lock we have to look elsewhere—to the great Kingdom of the Nile.

The sickle-shaped key was used in Egypt long before there was an Assyrian Empire. We find it in a bas-relief on the columns of the great temple at Karnak, which was built about 2000 B.C. Other keys, some with iron pins and ivory handles, some inlaid with gold and silver, have been found in various tombs at Luxor. All these were intended for wooden locks. (The all-metal lock and metal key, generally of bronze although sometimes of iron, were Roman innovations.) So wooden locks had been in use among the Egyptians at least four thousand years ago, long before any other people had employed them.

What is remarkable about the Egyptian lock is that it operated on the principle of the pin tumbler, which, translated into steel or brass by Linus Yale, Jr., was responsible for his fine cylinder lock.

Charles Courtney, lock expert extraordinary, who in his lifetime opened chests and safes for kings and emperors, on land and in the holds of ships on the bottom of the sea, summed it up in his *Unlocking Adventure:*

The pyramid makers designed such a good lock that we haven't been able to think of a better basic idea to this day. All we have done is to go them one or two better in improvements. They fastened their doors with a long hollow bolt and staple made of wood, generally teak, the hardest they could find. Into the upper part of the staple or housing, they fitted several loose pins that dropped into matching holes in the bolt and held it in place. The key was a

French lock and key. Above: outside lock plate; below: inner works with quadruple bolts (right) operated by gears. Steel. 18th century. 9 x 15 x 2¼ in. John M. Mossman Collection of Locks and Keys, New York.

flat stick of wood, generally thirteen or fourteen inches long for a street door, with a peg on the end to correspond to the pins in the bolt. To unlock the door, the Egyptians stuck the key through a round hole in the wall, lifted the pins until they cleared the bolt, then drew back the bolt by pulling the key which held it by pegs sticking in the pinholes. Egyptian locksmiths carried their finished keys about on their shoulders like a bunch of fagots.

These keys were indeed large. "Keys for Egyptian locks," said John M. Mossman, "were, and are, thirteen or fourteen inches long, whereas the key of the gate of a public building was sometimes two feet in length. A great deal of importance was attached to these keys. They were the signs of authority and were carried on the shoulder. . . ."

Wooden locks were also used in other Near East countries. They still are not uncommon in Morocco, in the Congo, in the East Indies, in the Moluccas

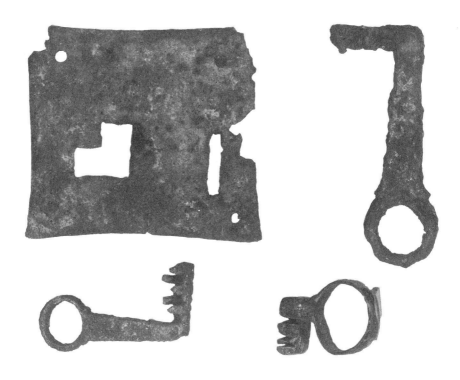

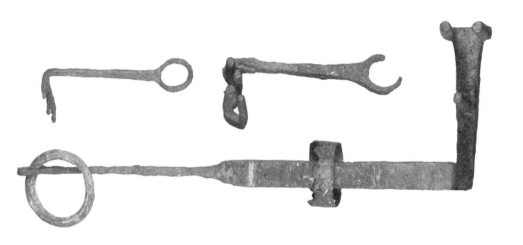

Above and below: Coptic keys found at Luxor. Bronze. Ca. 5th–8th century. Largest
12 in. long.
Opposite: Roman keys and lock plate found in Holy Land. Largest key iron, others
bronze. Ca. 2nd century. John M. Mossman Collection of Locks and Keys, New
York.

Above: Roman padlocks. Bronze 1st–3rd century. The British Museum, London.

Opposite: American percussion cap lock. Insertion of intruder's key caused cap to explode. Gas-escape hole in rim. Steel. 19th century. Yale & Towne Lock Collection.

and Tanimbar islands specifically, and in South America, at Surinam.

Vincent J. M. Eras, the Dutch authority, observed that these wooden locks "have square sliding blocks, and their keys are provided with corresponding square notches to operate and set these blocks. . . ." He noted that similar wooden locks were used in the Faeroe Islands, and that others had been seen in the Scottish Lowlands, Germany, France and Belgium. Mr. Eras observed that wooden locks are preferred in damp regions where iron locks will rust. That would explain why shelter huts in the Alps are fitted with wooden locks even today.

In central and eastern Europe, including Russia, in the countries of equatorial Africa, and in Mexico and Peru, researchers may still find remarkable wooden locks, and iron locks, too, that may be centuries old. Indeed, the whole

subject of wooden locks deserves further investigation and research by scholars
and collectors.

The keys that we call Coptic are, of course, Egyptian. The Copts, from the
third to sixth or seventh centuries, were the Christians of Egypt. However,
their keys are so much like the Romans' that they may be incorrectly identified.
Yet there is a different quality in the Coptic bronze that the practiced eye will
discern. Furthermore, Coptic keys, like those found in Luxor, are grosser than
the Roman. Their bows frequently are no more than ordinary circlets, not as
pleasing as the Roman. But, as might be expected, the Coptic are by far the
scarcer keys.

Roman ring keys from Pompeii. Center: shank and bit swivel, key can be concealed in palm. Bronze. Before 79 A.D. Schlage Antique Lock Collection, San Francisco.

CHAPTER IV

Once More the Romans

"You shall not now be stolen: you have locks upon you."
—*Cymbeline*

ABOUT THREE THOUSAND YEARS AGO, the Phoenicians, those traveling sales-men of antiquity, are said to have brought the wooden pinlock that Egypt invented and her craftsmen produced for commerce, to the shores of Cornwall. Perhaps the Phoenicians traded the wooden locks for some of the precious tin ore from the Cornish hills; that tin, combined in a ratio of one to ten with copper from Cyprus or Sinai, made the bronze alloy that was the most ser-viceable of metals prior to the regular smelting of iron ores.

The Britons copied the pinlocks in the native oakwoods. They made them so sturdily that the types remained in use in the west of England and in the north in Scotland until Victorian craftsmen began to fashion locks in metal.

However, the thousands of Roman keys available in collections bear testi-mony that it was the Romans who developed locks and keys and popularized their use. Many of these keys were heirlooms in early accumulations of antique objects treasured by the Renaissance princes of ruling houses. Others were ex-cavated more recently, notably from Pompeii, Herculaneum and other historic sites across the continent that great Rome ruled.

It is curious that so few Roman locks survived. Indeed, they are so rare that we know little about them. We do know that the Romans introduced a spring to press the pins into the bolt, and that they also invented the wards. From the steps in the bits, we assume that in later times the Roman locks had wards to foil the wrong keys or picklocks. Such pins as have been found are in different shapes, indicating that the Romans came to realize the importance of making *different* mechanisms that could not all be worked by a single key.

Occasionally, in an encrusted mass, a padlock has been found, for the Romans apparently favored loose, portable locks. So many Roman keys had little projections on the bow that we deduce that many of their locks had key-hole guards that were pushed or turned away by these metal teats. Because the bits are often like little pitchforks with tines turned at a ninety-degree angle, we also know that some Roman keys, like the Chinese padlocks they may have inspired, slid forward into the locks to open them, rather than rotating in the keyholes.

Why have so few Roman locks been found? First, many were of iron and rusted hopelessly underground into formless masses, or corroded into lumps that were easier thrown into the melting crucible than treated carefully, as the modern conservator is trained to do.

Second, Rome was destroyed slowly in one barbarian invasion after another. Her marbles were burned for lime, or were incorporated into newer structures, and later architects built over vast fields of rubble that would be treasure troves for today's sharp-eyed archeological students. Locks, always valuable, were carried away by invaders and other predators. Many, no doubt, are still on doors and on coffers where either they have been ignored or simply have not been recognized for what they are.

Romans, so practical a people, fostered and demanded every instrument or device that made living privately more comfortable. Locks and keys must have protected many fine residences, offices, warehouses and important military posts. Regrettably, we have few to examine and study.

Roman bronze or iron-and-bronze keys occur both with rings at the bow for carrying on the finger and with volutes at the bow for carrying on a riband or a chain, or with other keys on a large metal circlet. Unlike modern keys, which are flat, the bits on Roman keys often turn a ninety-degree angle either on a plane with the shank or perpendicular to it.

They were made in various sizes, from keys for the little finger to some as large as the ceremonial keys conferred on state visitors in our time. Frequently, the bits were cut like a meander or a labyrinth. In the bronze, now patinated green, they are not unattractive. Once the eye has fixed upon their pattern they are not difficult to identify.

Because Roman garments had no pockets, small Roman keys were often attached to finger rings. Many of the rings of small diameter must have been made for women. A pity that none can be identified as one that Julius Caesar wore, or that Brutus had on his fist when he raised the fatal dagger, or that the philosopher Seneca slipped from his hand before he stepped into his bath to open his veins and take his life at Nero's cruel command. Probably few Romans of high rank wore keys, although there are "key rings" that once contained carved intaglios of carnelian, sard or jasper in the bezel, and so must have been worn by senators or other wealthy men. Most of the large keys, carried loose or on great circlets, were entrusted to stewards and chamberlains, or to the mistresses of the Roman households.

Occasionally, a key appears that is truly a transitional object, indelibly from the culture of one period but already showing the influence of another. Such is the extraordinary Ptolemaic key from the Lips Collection in Holland, which is bronze and flat, clearly Egyptian, yet somewhat Roman in character. The bow is high; the inner frame, rectangular like an Egyptian gate, is the sistrum headdress over the head of Hathor the goddess, with her heifer ears and hair visible. The flat shank, engraved with a royal cartouche, gives in hieroglyphics the name of Ptolemy II Philadelphus who ruled 283–246 B.C. The bit, which sits at right angles, also has the shepherd's flail that the kings carried, and the ankh sign.

Artistically, this is the finest key known from Egypt, and is said to have been made to unlock a sarcophagus. The Ptolemies, of course, were Greek, descendants of Ptolemy I, the general whom Alexander of Macedon left to rule on the Nile. In the period when some anonymous craftsman created this key the Romans, already a power in the Mediterranean, were at war with Carthage. More than two centuries would pass before Caesar and Marc Antony would, in turn, claim Cleopatra, but Roman craftsmanship, at least Roman influence, seems evident here.

Dredging in the rivers of the Netherlands has brought up many fine Roman keys. More have turned up in Italy, of course, and also in Germany, France and Spain. Many more can be expected as new excavations are made in the Balkans, eastern and central Europe, and the Levant. One day, Roman locks may be found in a state of excellent preservation. Since the Romans favored padlocks, some in simple barrel forms, others more ornamental, with decorative facings although with heavy shackles, some of these can certainly be expected from various excavations. Also, strongboxes with sliding lids and multiple fastenings, much like modern locked chests, may be uncovered. One need not look only for simply made keys. Many will have flourishes and leafy designs, and perhaps even such elegant work as the little bust of a child that graces the bow of a particularly splendid example illustrated on page 7.

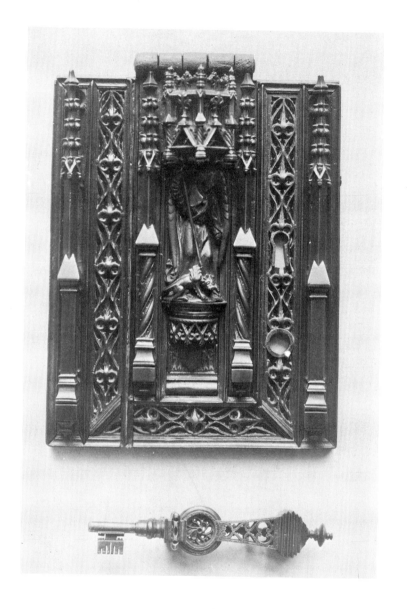

French Gothic key and door lock with St. Michael and the Devil. Figures slide out to expose keyhole. Iron and steel. 15th century. Key: 6 in.; lock: 9¾ x 7¼ in. City Art Museum of St. Louis.

CHAPTER V

The Nature of Gothic

"Mistletoe acts as a master-key as well as a lightning conductor; for it
is said to open all locks." —*The Golden Bough,* James G. Frazer

ALL-METAL LOCKS appeared between the years 870 and 900. The first were
said to have been made in England during the reign of Alfred the Great, who
was an admirer of fine locks. Fitted in or around the keyhole were all sorts of
wards or obstructions to make the locks secure against tampering. If all-metal
locks indeed originated in England, it is not known precisely when the C -
tinent began to produce them, but it probably was not much later than e
tenth century.

There is a general carelessness in classifying locks and keys from the Roman
period to the Renaissance epoch. The words "Medieval" or "Gothic" are used
loosely to cover our ignorance of the precise qualities that differentiate the
objects made from the third or fourth centuries to the early fifteenth. With due
caution, some guidance may be offered.

"Medieval" is such a catchall term that it is not very helpful, and should perhaps be avoided. Locks and keys called "Merovingian" relate to the time of
Merowig, the founder of the Frankish dynasty in Europe which ruled from
about 500 to 751. Those identified as "Carolingian" are attributable to the
Frankish kings who ruled in France 751–987, in Germany 752–911, in Italy
774–961. The period is named after Carolus Magnus, the Charles the Great
whom we know better as Charlemagne, king of France 768–814, Emperor of
the West 800–814.

"Gothic" covers the era from the middle of the twelfth century to the early
fifteenth, when the exuberant Renaissance influence began to assert itself. The
Gothic style of architecture was characterized by slender vertical piers and
buttresses balanced by pointed arches and vaulting. It began in northern
France and spread through western Europe. Its influence was notable in the
design of locks and keys.

It is not easy to separate the Merovingian from the Carolingian keys. The
Merovingian give the impression of being less compact in structure than the

Roman. The shanks often end in pins, the bits are coarser, the bows simpler. Definitely they are, with exceptions, less forceful than the Roman works. (Why there should have been such a loss in craftsmanship might be an interesting subject for study.)

Keys of the Carolingian period often have bows in the shape of a bishop's miter, either clearly so or with modifications, like those on page 39. They are generally flat, and of bronze, and nearly all give a feeling of latticework or present the profile of a chair. Occasionally, the bits end in animal heads. Sometimes the bows are engraved with medieval dotted patterns, or leaves. Like the Merovingian, the Carolingian are far less common than Roman keys.

The Gothic keys of bronze or iron are more elaborate. The bows are diamond- or lozenge-shaped. Another variation is the diamond lozenge quartered into four diamonds. The keys are generally flat and the steps in the bits indicate that wards were used around the keyholes. They always remind one of the dignity of Gothic edifices, especially of the belfries and spires and the stained-glass windows. Occasionally, a key folds over by means of a freely moving rivet.

In the Gothic period, too, there is no noticeable advance in lock construction over the Roman era. The first door-locks of the Gothic period had horizontal keyholes rather than vertical ones. The horizontal placement kept the mechanism simpler; no extra lever was necessary to actuate the small bolts inside which slid up and down. But the horizontal keyhole was not in harmony with the exterior design, and some time later a craftsman wearied of it, and changed it to the vertical position.

There were no spring locks, that is, locks that locked themselves when the door was closed. Such were not made until the middle of the sixteenth century, with the Renaissance well under way. More time was spent on concealing the keyhole and the latch with special covers and devices. That effort was to continue until concealment became a fine art in the seventeenth century.

Yet German, Italian and French locksmiths of the Gothic period, with the comparatively simple tools available to them, produced excellent locks. In 1411, Charles IV of Germany established the title of Master Locksmith, a sufficient indication of the high esteem with which the craftsman was now

French Carolingian keys. Iron. 8th–10th century. Musée le Secq des Tournelles, Rouen. Note bishop's miter style.

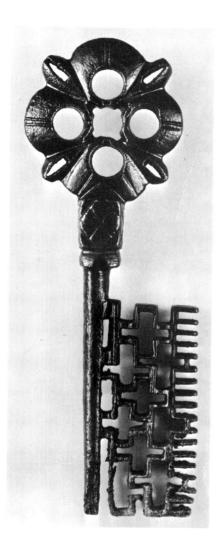

Above: French Carolingian key: petaled bow, latticed bit. Iron. 8th–10th century. Right: French Merovingian key: high open crown in bow, latticed bit. Iron. 6th–8th century. National Museum (Bargello), Florence.

regarded. If the internal works showed no significant improvement, the decoration on the lock cases became increasingly pleasing.

The fourteenth century saw further elaboration of the Gothic style, with a great variety in the fenestrations in the bows. The wards multiplied until they were like closely placed iron stairs.

In the thirteenth and fourteenth centuries the Gothic lock cases offered fine wrought ironwork, with ornaments inspired by animal or vegetable forms, and lilies, roses and thistles predominating. As Otto Hoever noted, "Ornament in smithcraft depended on the decorative designs invented by the draughtsman. In the Gothic period, the smiths chiefly drew their inspiration from illuminated manuscripts." In the late Gothic period, the iron craftsmen turned from illumination to calligraphic ornament.

The early smith had worked his iron while it was hot. He cut his ingots into bars, and he pounded his bars into sheets. He lived with his metal through the long workday, and pursued it until he had made the rough shapes. He developed a facility for handling the metal on his anvil from a near-glowing incandescence to various stages of red, and forced it to his will with swift and repeated blows. He heated and reheated, hammered and rehammered, alone or with the aid of journeymen and apprentices, and caused the iron to assume the temper and to reach the quality he desired. He was proud of the metal and proud that he was its master. He forged, he embossed, he tinned or gilded when required, and he added ornamentation or damascening. Like the armorer, he engraved or chased, or etched—or turned over the work to those who were better qualified for such special applications.

Among the finest lock artists were men like Jorg Heusz, famous also as the Master Clockmaker of Nürnberg in 1449, and Hans Ehemann, also of Nürnberg, reported to be the inventor of the letter ring combination padlock. Smiths of their reputation were internationally famous and were invited to make master locks and keys for the courts of France and Italy, too, which is one reason why the presence of a lock or key in a given country cannot be taken as an assumption that it was produced there.

CHAPTER VI

Renaissance

"Love laughs at locksmiths."

IT WOULD BE SURPRISING if the Renaissance did not inspire locksmiths as it did craftsmen and artists in every other field. We are compelled to dwell on the keys because there were still no unusual improvements in either the design or the construction of the locks.

A change had taken place in the activities of the locksmith: he no longer worked the iron hot. He was in control now: he needed the forge less, and used the file, the cold chisel and the saw with extraordinary dexterity. The change, which came at the end of the fifteenth century, was to alter the esthetic character of the key. Free from his dependence on the heat of the metal, the smith no longer had to work rapidly. He could proceed slowly and dwell on details. He would lose the vigor of the best of the forged Gothic work, but he would, at the risk of affectation, have the liberty to elaborate. The Renaissance key was the result.

The "business" end of the Renaissance key—the bit—elaborately incised though it may be, it is still comparatively plain. The ornately embellished part of the key is now at the bow; and it is the bow that, with uncanny precision, usually expresses the spirit of its epoch.

This is charmingly confirmed by the *clefs de chef-d'oeuvre,* the masterpiece keys, in France, made between 1550 and 1650. (Compare these to the keys made in France a century earlier to see their prototypes. The latter, of course, cruder in execution, are the more vigorous and artistic.) Before any journeyman could be accepted by the Guild of Locksmiths as a master, he was required to submit at least one superbly carved lock and key. These masterpieces were not for actual use, but to demonstrate a man's skill with chisel, saw and file. The masterpiece keys were kept either on display in the guildhall or by the master locksmith in his forge or atelier.

English key with St. George slaying the dragon. Forged steel. 17th century. Lips Collection, Dordrecht.

From the late sixteenth to the late eighteenth centuries, the bows of these keys were large and, in many cases, in the form of an inverted pyramid over a ring form copied from the Gothic window and enriched with traceries. Borrowing their designs from cathedral architecture, the smiths composed keys in the form of beautiful towers or turrets, and elaborate windows with pinwheels, spirals and foliations, all produced from cold steel not at the forge but at the bench.

A small masterpiece key, gracefully proportioned, has a little rounded steel window plus a finial on top; others with similar windows have crisscrossed ribs plus a tower in which sinuous lines climb upward, or hexagonal open pavilions, or towers plus carved figures on top instead of ordinary finials (see pages 44 and 63). Never before or after this time were keys made so proudly. The silence of the vaulted cathedral is captured in steel compositions. Spire and arch, gable and niche, cusp and tendril are wedded here. So tightly woven are the elements that the eye finds itself peering into shadows and, while enjoying the lacelike metal, imagines processionals.

Examine these keys under magnification. Hammer has tapped and chisel has cut and file has smoothed until each piece is as butter-smooth is if it had been molded. This is true of fine keys in every period, much more so of these masterwork keys which, unlike the Roman or Gothic keys, have no green patina but wear their original silvery coats. Although not intended for use, they came under the scrutiny of master locksmiths and so had to pass the severest tests. Though a hundred corners and crevices were worked and turned, each was required to be without flaw. We know that they were carved, yet the critical eye continues to search for evidence that they were cast. The surfaces of a few were incised with appropriate arabesques, or were damascened with inlays of silver and gold.

On many, the shanks are unusually short and the bits below appear disproportionately large. The steps are piled one above the other like the teeth in a comb. Indeed, the best of these little works of art, which are of French workmanship, were called *clefs à peigne,* or "comb keys."

The Italian masters never equaled their northern neighbors. Often Italian keys were not carved from single bars of metal, but were assembled from

French masterpiece key with warded bit and elaborate bow including pavilion, scrolled window and box capital. Steel. 16th century. The Metropolitan Museum of Art, New York, Gift of Giulia Morosini, 1932.

Above: European lock, perhaps French, with St. John the Baptist over hinged key-hole. Iron. 15th or 16th century. 5½ x 4¼ in. The Metropolitan Museum of Art, New York, Cloisters Collection.

Opposite below: English door lock made for Henry VIII by royal locksmith Henry Romayne, with orb and crown over Tudor rose. (Modern screw tops.) Formerly, Horace Walpole collection at Strawberry Hill. Steel. Ca. 1530. Walters Art Gallery, Baltimore: Above: Spanish chest lock with masks and unusual full-length figure on hasp. Steel. Late 15th century. The Hispanic Society of America, New York.

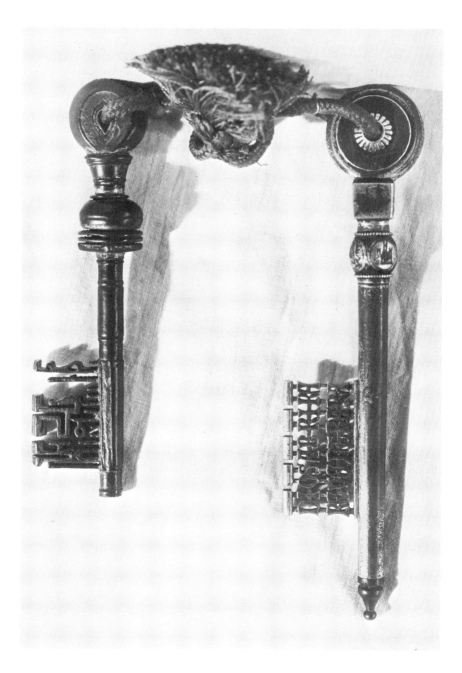

neatly fitted pieces. These, although cleverly contrived, are less worthy of praise. Even casual examination reveals that the ribs in the little windows sometimes are of copper; even when of steel, the ribs are grafts, incorporated by brazing, and not elements chiseled from the ingot, and so they lack that organic unity of the French keys.

German keys are generally superior to the Italian, but, though often vigorous in design, are not up to the mark set by the French artisans. Spanish keys are cumbersome; where they are finer, one may assume that they were made by French smiths.

Fifteenth-century locks express themselves by splendidly chiseled, and applied, ornamentation. The front of the lock was divided into little compartments, with pinnacles above and the buttresses and traceries that distinguished the earlier Gothic architecture. Every detail was cut, or sawn, or chiseled from iron. In the greatest locks, layers of ornamentation were cunningly applied one upon the other. Often, behind, or underneath, is fine red velvet to supply a rich contrasting backdrop.

The best are French. The German locksmiths sometimes equaled French work. The two are not always easy to tell apart, except that the French locks are rectangular and many of the German locks, with less of the fine sawn and chiseled work, have outlines that permit generous curves to splay outward. The Germans devised extremely complicated locks for the inside of coffers, with many bolts shooting out in every direction to insure greater security.

Spain's great cathedrals, modified by the Moorish heritage of the peninsula, have their own solemn airs; her craftsmen were equal to any in Europe. Her best smiths, however, were occupied with such large ironwork projects as the great altar screens, and their locks and keys cannot be compared to the best French work, although many of their heavy padlocks are impressive.

Two twelfth-century Moorish keys from the Cathedral of Seville, the larger of gilded bronze, the smaller of iron, are alleged to be the keys that were formally surrendered to King Ferdinand III when the Moors yielded the great city in 1248. The smaller key has an Arabic inscription which has been trans-

Left: Gilded Moorish key yielded to Ferdinand III by Axataf when Seville capitulated in 1248. Bit with cursive Islamic legend. 12th century. Right: Spanish key with arms of Castile and Leon on shoulder and unusual bit with Latin legend. Treasury of Seville Cathedral, photo courtesy MAS, Barcelona.

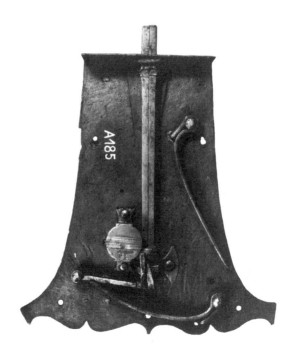

Above: German masterpiece key in ward housing, with Moor's head decoration. Steel. Probably 17th century. Bavarian National Museum, Munich.

Opposite: German chest lock, front and back views. Iron. 16th century. German National Museum, Nürnberg.

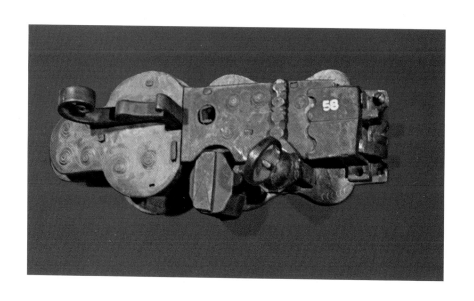

lated as "To God all empire and power." The Aragonese key of the fourteenth century, on page 48, carries a Latin inscription.

Fifteenth-century Spanish locks, flamboyant in design, with keyholes concealed and vertical panels traceried, might pass for the products of any other European country except for the attention paid to the decorations on the fixing staples that held knocker or lock box in place. These staples were often disguised with pillars that bore figures like caryatids, or even with heads to mask the bolts in the corners.

Excellent metalwork was done in embellishing the popular type of chest known as the Varqueño. Though braces, plaques and other metal trimmings were skillfully employed, it is the charmingly executed lock and hasp that represent Spain's distinctive contribution to artistic lockmaking in this period.

COLOR PLATE II   Top: Swedish castle lock. Steel. 14th century. Bottom: Russian padlock and key owned by Ivan the Terrible (1530–1584). Steel. Schlage Antique Lock Collection, San Francisco.

CHAPTER VII

Padlocks

"Gold be a key for every lock."—John Lyly

PADLOCKS MAY HAVE BEEN IN USE long before locks were fixed permanently inside doors, drawers or chests. With metal expensive and few craftsmen to work it, the padlock was a practical item since it could be carried about and used wherever needed, on a portmanteau, a strongbox or a treasury door. Padlocks were forged in every size, from the tiny ones of platinum, which a Siberian exile made for the pleasure of the Empress Catherine the Great, to stout, massive ones, like the Ivan the Terrible padlock, to great, clumsy affairs that weighed up to twenty pounds and were applied to huge coffers.

Though crude, rugged and even impressive, padlocks were hardly burglar-proof. A heavy tool could force open the shackle or wrench away the supporting hasp and staple and the padlock with it. This loose hanging lock was not called a "padlock" because it saved possessions from footpads. The name derived from the English provincial "pad" or "pod" for a pannier or basket; the padlock was the lock for a basket in which goods or provisions were taken to market. ("Pedlar" or "peddler" is from the same root.)

Whatever the etymology, the padlock was hammered out to be used rather than admired. As Edgar B. Frank, author of *Old French Ironwork: The Craftsman and His Art,* put it, "Padlocks never enjoyed the esteem with which fixed locks were regarded, and almost always remained the latters' poor relations. Few indeed are to be found whose mechanisms, as well as whose decorations, approached those of regular locks."

The fundamental construction of the padlock was dictated by its purpose. A hanging lock must have a shackle from which to hang. Except for the Chinese padlocks, some Byzantine padlocks, and a few Spanish padlocks, the

German padlock and key. Steel. 17th century. Key: 8⅛ in.; lock: 6¼ in. Bavarian National Museum, Munich.

Above: German padlock with key inserted. Steel. 17th or 18th century. Lock: 6 5/16 x 7 7/8 x 3 15/16 in.
Opposite: German padlock and key. Steel. 17th or 18th century. Lock: 7 1/2 x 4 3/4 in.
Bavarian National Museum, Munich.

shackles were usually curved and were hinged to the locks.

The shape of the lock varied. The ball, or spherical, shape was always popular. That was true also for the square or oblong shape. To appeal to customers, locksmiths created many quaint shapes. The heart was favored, rounded or pointed. Some were oval like acorns or curved like shields; some were triangular.

Mechanically, the padlocks had few parts and were put together simply. The wards around the keyhole were not complicated. The padlock could not for long thwart any determined picklock.

The men who made locks knew it, although in the early centuries, with the knowledge of tools and devices rather limited, the padlock needed only the appearance of security. The nimble-fingered, however, gave them reason to

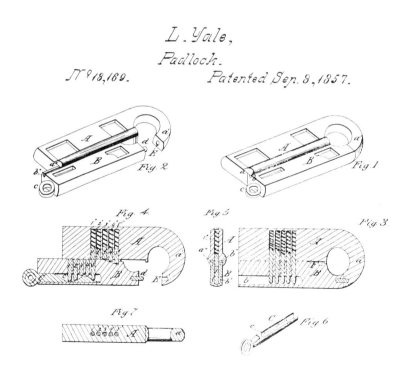

L. Yale,
Padlock.
№ 18,169.
Patented Sep. 8, 1857.

seek to improve these locks. They faltered at reconstructing the interiors, but they did make serious efforts to conceal the keyholes. Often the modes of concealment were cleverer than the works inside. A secret pin or rivet must be depressed, or some scroll be thrust aside, or a key unlock a cover plate under which the important keyhole had been hidden.

A logical development now was the padlock that did not depend on keys and keyholes but operated by combinations of letters or numbers on revolving disks of metal. The correct combination required the alignment of the several disks so that they were in a specific order, and thus released the catch and permitted the lock to open. Whether the combination was in Roman letters or in the cursive Persian, the combination lock conveyed an air of mystery, as it still does. The problem with combinations is that when they are long or complex

Opposite: Original patent application sketches of Linus Yale, Sr.'s five-pin-tumbler padlock; model shown below. Yale & Towne Lock Collection.

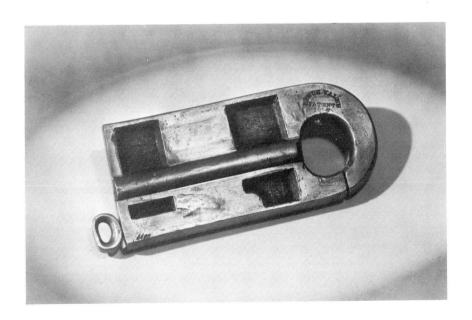

the owner of the lock may forget them. Simple combinations, however, have always been popular.

The Chinese brass padlock operates on a principle that may have been borrowed from the Romans. The key, which is a narrow bar, square in cross section, does not turn to open the lock. Instead it slides in all the way and, with this action, depresses the springs which, by being expanded, have been holding the two parts of the lock together. Disengaged now by the entrance of the key, the lock can be pulled apart and thus opened.

Some padlocks had keys that were threaded. Screw the key in, and the shackle is released. Some padlocks had shackles that were not hinged but came out entirely. While the majority of padlocks were simple, many were not. Some Spanish and French padlocks of the seventeenth century had twin shackles with twin mechanisms. Others concealed the keyholes behind secret little doors recessed into the faces of the locks. Still others had secret buttons that must be pushed before the key could be inserted.

The padlocks that were crafted for royalty, or for the nobility, or for wealthy merchants, were often lavishly tooled. Sometimes the metal surfaces were inlaid with gold and silver or damascened in splendid style. Little padlocks in the forms of animals were regarded as fetching, sure to please a lady or a favored child. In India, locks in the forms of little figures were common.

Secure or not, the padlock is still in use. Today, while the shackle may still be its weak point, the modern padlock is far superior to its predecessors. One of the finest employs the pin-tumbler principle, borrowed from the ancient Egyptians but executed in hardened metals to make as handsome and tamper-proof a device as can be expected in a lock of this type.

No lock has as long and diversified a history as the padlock. Once it guarded a man's chest of valuables; it secured the gates of his castle; it kept fast the doors of his prison or dungeon keep, and it closed the shackles on the irons that bound his slaves. It was also the padlock on the *ceinture de chasteté,* or *keuschheitsgürtel,* that incredible device made of leather, silver or iron, that we know as "the chastity girdle," which the lord compelled his wife to wear

Indian lock for temple cabinet, with gold and silver inlays. Turban conceals keyway and unscrews to admit pin-shaped key. Brass. Probably 18th century. Schlage Antique Lock Collection, San Francisco.

Es S Mag Passien

MELCHIOR. SCHEDEL.

about her loins while he went off to war or crusade.

An illustration of the coat of arms of sixteenth-century Melchior Schedel displays the knight clad in a combination of armor and courtly raiment facing his lady, who is naked except for the cross at her bosom and the chastity girdle around her loins. She obligingly carries in her hand the huge key that will open the padlock sitting on her hip. Perhaps it was such an ironic depiction that inspired that urbane aphorism "Love laughs at locksmiths."

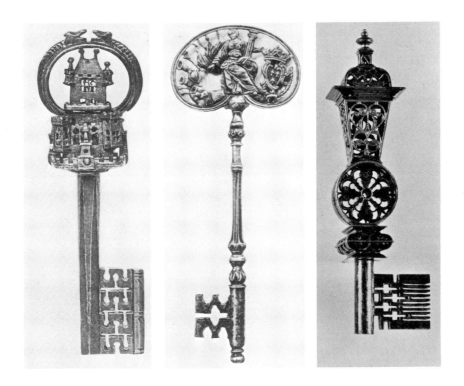

Above left: German key with château-fortress in bow. Steel. 16th century. Center: English key with a Virtue and coat of arms. Steel. 17th or 18th century. Musée le Secq des Tournelles, Rouen. Right: French masterpiece key. Steel. 16th century. National Museum (Bargello), Florence.

Opposite: 16th century woodcut of Melchior Schedel's coat of arms, showing woman wearing chastity girdle and holding key in her hand. From *Illustrierte Sittengeschichte: Renaissance* by Eduard Fuchs.

English early "detector" lock, signed by John Wilkes of Birmingham and inscribed with cautionary verse. Dial, right, registers number of times lock has been opened. Steel. Ca. 1700. Victoria and Albert Museum, London.

CHAPTER VIII

On the Eve of the Industrial Age

"My name is Chubb, that makes the Patent Locks:
Look on my works, ye burglars, and despair."
—from a humorous sonnet in *Tait's Magazine* (London) April, 1841

ENGLISH LOCKS AND KEYS came into their own in the early eighteenth century. After literally dominating the European market, the French began to make keys with bronze bows. Suddenly, English keys of steel, always graceful and light enough to be carried, became popular on the Continent, and even in France. At their best, the English keys were delightfully executed. They seemed to radiate self-assurance and elegance. The bows offered ciphers or monograms, sometimes with crowns or coronets, sometimes with coats of arms, always tastefully scrolled. The shanks were lathe-turned to match the style of the bows and the steps in the bits. The surface polish was brilliant.

In the competition between England and France, the locksmiths of the latter were not to be ignored. If the French product was no longer unique, it still had admirers. The cool charm of the Louis XIV period is evident in keys that are superbly chased, or are dainty, or are gilded or engraved. However, place them side by side and the English key stands out, almost smugly so, in the work of this period.

When fine English locks appeared, in the late seventeenth and eighteenth century, they were usually of steel but had brass cases with engraved or applied ornaments. The period of Adam furniture brought new refinements in the locks and lock plates required to harmonize with the Neoclassic style.

The era of important locks and keys did not end with the ornate, splendidly decorated objects of the French and the English masters. On the contrary, very important locks and keys—from point of view of efficiency—began to be made only after the ornate ones were no longer being produced.

When did the locksmith begin to turn his attention to a redesigning of the inner works rather than a refurbishing of the outer design? On the eve of the Industrial Revolution—or was it already in full swing?—the utilitarians were taking over. The English locksmith Joseph Bramah, here celebrated as a lock inventor, made improvements in the steam engine and sued James Watts. He invented a machine for making quill pen points and also a hydraulic press, and for a while considered his fine lock as only a side effort from his workshop. One of the great innovators, he contributed significantly to make the modern lock blandly simple in its exterior, its strength concealed within.

"Wherever there is a keyhole a lock can be picked." So said Albert A. Hopkins, summing up his experience as a student of the locks and keys in the famous John M. Mossman Collection on which his book, *The Lure of the Lock,* was based. Mossman, designer and architect of some of the largest burglarproof and fireproof bank vaults in the United States, had been in the safe-and-lock business since the age of twelve. At the time of his death in 1912, his collection of locks and keys was the largest in existence, including the most modern combination and time locks, which European collectors had up to then ignored.

Hopkins concluded that any picklock who can get a tool into a keyhole will, sooner or later, discover how the device works and succeed in opening it. That was why the locksmiths of the sixteenth and seventeenth centuries masked the keyhole with escutcheons that could be lifted only by secret pins and by many marvelously attractive yet innocent-looking obstacles. That was why locksmiths often used an auxiliary lock to block the main keyhole. The great Gothic and Renaissance locks, for all their handsome facades that make them so attractive to museums and collectors, provided little security. Fortunately, lock-picking had not yet become a fine art. When it did, new inventors hastily sought to strengthen the inner mechanisms.

In 1778, Robert Barron of England obtained a patent for a lock that no longer depended on wards around the keyhole, although it did retain them. He had two spring tumblers of different sizes checking the bolt, with notches in the tail of the bolt to correspond to these tumblers. The latter were lifted by the various cuts in the bit of the key. At the correct levels the bolt was released and could be moved. This twin-tumbler lock was a great advance over its predecessors. The key looked simple; its steps were like those on earlier keys. But with its wards and tumblers, the lock was relatively complicated.

Joseph Bramah, who patented the first of his many new lock mechanisms in 1784, was fortunate that a wave of sensational burglaries sweeping England forced the public to consider his product. He devised a system of sliders with notches in different positions. One part of the slider was recessed in the mechanism, the other sat in a fixed ring with notches. Only by inserting the key could the notches in the sliders be adjusted to fit with the projections of the ring, and only when everything so coincided was the mechanism freed so that the key could be turned. When the key was removed, spiral openings at the end of each slider caused the parts by their own gravity to drop back into place. Where the Barron lock had required merely a simple rotating movement inside, the Bramah lock utilized endways pushing of the sliding bars inside, as well as a revolving movement. The Bramah, incidentally, was the first lock to be operated by a small key that could be carried around conveniently.

"Impregnable as the Rock of Gibraltar," was the Bramah slogan. Proud of his achievements, which included the first effective plan to manufacture lock parts in quantities and thus launched a lockmaking industry, Bramah, in 1811, offered two hundred guineas to "the artist who can make an instrument that will pick or open this lock." The offer gave Bramah locks wide publicity.

English burglars were equal to the new designs. After a particularly daring burglary in Portsmouth, accomplished by lock-picking, the government offered one hundred pounds to anyone who could construct a lock that could not be opened except by the authorized key. The records do not indicate that the prize was paid out, but Charles and Jeremiah Chubb came forward with their Detector Lock, patented in 1818, that, for a while, baffled the lock-pickers. All the Chubb brothers, Charles, Jeremiah and John, contributed improvements, and their lever design was popularly accepted.

The levers consisted of brass strips and formed the elements that checked the bolt. These levers swung on a pivot that was riveted to the lock case and were kept down by spring action. Precision was demanded in the construction of the levers, the springs, the bolt and the gating, which is a slot in the lever. The security depended on the precision with which the stump on the bolt-tail passed through the gating and the pocket. By varying the number of levers, and also varying the wards of the lock and the steps in the bit of the key, endless numbers of locks and keys could be made, each different, each fairly secure against picking and tampering.

Other locksmiths made contributions, each another step forward in the security of the householder and the banker. The competition among the lockmakers was severe, with challenges flung—and accepted. In May, 1832, Thomas Hart, locksmith of Wolverhampton, the center of English lockmaking, challenged one of the Chubb locks. Charles Chubb put up ten pounds against him. But time was called on Hart before he could complete his lockpicking.

It remained for Alfred C. Hobbs, an American expert, sometime salesman of fireproof safes, attending the International Industrial Exhibition in London in 1851, to win the prizes. With his lock-picking tools, Hobbs opened first a Bramah and then a Chubb lock at the Crystal Palace within twenty-five minutes. Bramah felt that he must stand on his, by now, forty-year-old reward offer. Under the supervision of an arbitration committee, Hobbs went to work on a splendid Bramah padlock. After several days, he opened that lock, too, and, though Bramah protested, the two hundred guineas were paid over.

Hobbs made a good thing of vexing the British lockmakers. He is said also to have picked a Cotterill lock. Cotterill profited by adding a "detector" and

Below: Yale Double Treasury Bank Lock, by Linus Yale, Jr., with eight lever tumblers and two keys. Steel. Before 1862.
Opposite: Lips Protector key and lock. When unlocked, it is removed from keyhole for access to main lock. Steel. Early 20th century. John L. Mossman Collection of Locks and Keys, New York.

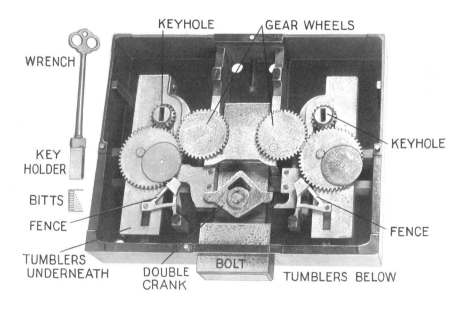

patenting his lock mechanism as the "Patent Climax-Detector" lock. The principles were those used in the Bramah lock except that the spring-loaded sliders
were positioned at right angles to the notches in the key. The detector, if jolted
by a false key or picking tool, fell into place in such a way that only the proper
key inserted and turned to shoot the bolt could restore it to its resting position.
Chubb later devised a detector lock that was more effective than Cotterill's.

Hobbs, incidentally, having given British locksmiths a bad time, founded his
own lock and safe company and stayed on in England for thirty years. In 1854,
one of Chubb's workmen successfully picked one of Hobbs' patent Protector
locks. He had studied it for months and fashioned special tools to pick it, but
his accomplishment did seem to vindicate British honor, if not workmanship.

American latch lock from Pennsylvania. Wrought iron. Mid-18th century. Overall: 9⅛ in.; "key" handle: 4½ in.; strike plate: 2½ in. The Metropolitan Museum of Art, New York, Gift of Mrs. J. Insley Blair, 1949.

CHAPTER IX

New World Ingenuity

» "A man's home is his castle."

THE EARLIEST HABITATIONS erected on the eastern seaboard had no locks, for they were cave dwellings or dugouts of earth and sod, fashioned hurriedly until the colonists could chop down trees and raise log houses.

On Manhattan Island the settlers' first dwellings were of bark, the sheets pinned on wooden frames. The first log cabins had dirt floors and bark doors. When the newcomers prospered, they built better houses, many furnished with goods imported from Great Britain. It was a long time, however, before doors were hung on iron hinges instead of on leather straps, and walls and roofs were made with nails throughout. Iron was so dear that the Virginia government offered any planter who abandoned a house as many nails as he had put into its framing to keep him from burning it down for sake of the original nails!

Doors on fine houses had latches with strings hanging outside. Pull the string through to the inside and it was securely locked. "The latch is out for you!" was a form of welcome.

When truly elegant homes were built they were more likely to have attractive door knockers than locks. The knockers were of wrought iron or polished brass. Except in houses that copied everything from English taste and so must be adorned with English hardware, knockers and door latches were forged by local smiths. Some of these, from New England and the Pennsylvania Dutch country, are as vigorous and attractive as any ever crafted by a German locksmith. They are sturdy and practical; no frills.

The colonists were not unequal to the forging of locks and keys. Many able clockmakers in seventeenth-century Boston, Philadelphia and New York built whole clocks from raw materials, often carving parts out of wood because brass was so expensive. Such clever craftsmen, and certainly the excellent gunsmiths of the late seventeenth and middle eighteenth centuries, were capable of constructing locks. But the colonists needed tools and implements for hinges, doors and shutters, fireplace and kitchen articles, lighting devices, and carriage parts. Locks were not needed. Even door latches were at the end of the want list.

The founding of the Republic in 1789 meant an end forever to dependence on England. Expansion westward brought an era of new prosperity. The self-reliant Yankee and Southern metalsmiths and tinkerers began to supply everything their neighbors were ready to pay for.

As ownership of valuables widened, the turbulent frontier society wanted security. Every man was free to carry a weapon, but he could not stay awake all night to guard his cashbox or his front door. Padlocks were now in demand. Strongboxes were needed. Town and city homes required sturdy locks. The Barron, the Bramah, the Chubb and the other British locks were relatively expensive, so the native craftsmen copied them and, in the ways of all inventive folk, tried their best to improve them.

Few signed their locks. Henry J. Kauffman, researching for his excellent *Early American Ironware: Cast and Wrought,* discovered less than a dozen signed locks, these chiefly out of the Lebanon area in the Pennsylvania Dutch country. The best were stamped or incised with the maker's name: Rohrer. "There seems to have been at least two generations of the family who signed locks," Kauffman wrote. The Rohrer locks, of the German type, were well-made, works a smith could be proud of, in the early decades of the nineteenth century and later. Doubtless hundreds of fine locks were made by American locksmiths who did not bother to stamp or to engrave their names or marks, and to whom it did not even occur to do so.

As early as 1836, Solomon Andrews of Perth Amboy, New Jersey, made it possible for the owner to change the position of the tumblers inside a lock. Ordinarily, such changes called for new keys. Andrews, however, ingeniously contrived a key on which the bits were movable, and could be shifted to match the changing of the tumblers. The owner merely had to make his tumbler rearrangements and shift the bits before he fixed the bolt. In theory, he could do this as often as he wished. But since it required dexterity, patience and at least a minimal knowledge of locks, the Andrews changeable lock was designed not for the homeowner, who would have found it difficult to manipulate, but for banks, to protect the large sums of coins and currency safeguarded within them. It tended to ensure at least that a glimpse of the key, which so often had been enough to give a picklock a head start, would be of no avail.

It is astonishing how much ingenuity was suddenly applied to lock mechanisms in the United States, much of it originally inspired by the products of the British locksmiths. Long before Solomon Andrews produced his changeable lock with its changeable bit, J. Perkins of Newbury, Massachusetts, had patented a massive, complicated burglarproof combination bank lock with a "key" of washers that could be rearranged whenever the owner pleased.

While Andrews was displaying his lock, Day and Newell of New York constructed a lock which was like his for its potential changes but had two sets of tumblers. When an American machinist won five hundred dollars for picking it, Newell redesigned it and produced the Parautoptic bank lock. The name (from the Greek for "hidden from sight") signified that it concealed its inner works so that a picklock could not explore it, and if he succeeded in getting in, the throw of a detector plate would close the keyhole. Incidentally, the Parautoptic received in 1847 a gold medal for its excellence from the National Mechanics' Institute of Lower Austria, no mean honor for an American invention.

In 1848, the Herring Company of New York produced a lock for fireproof safes for which the key was a semicircular piece of metal with teeth. Insert this little key in a depression left of the knob and turn handle to right. When the lock was unlocked, the key was ejected. The name "grasshopper" seemed natural for it.

Linus Yale, Sr., was not the first lockmaker to model a lock on the old Egyptian pin design, but he made the most effective modifications. To quote from Alfred C. Hobbs, his contemporary, he was combining "something like the Egyptian with something like the Bramah." As early as 1853, Hobbs, while describing it, seemed able to pick it, but apparently he admired it. It had two cylinders, one working within the other and held together by a series of pins reaching through the cylinders into the keyhole, which was in the center. The elder Yale began with four sets of pin tumblers, but, Hobbs noted, he could make them also with as many as forty pins. Except to a highly skilled picklock it, "would seem to present an insurmountable barrier."

Linus Yale, Jr., started his career as an artist and never really worked alongside his father, but he ultimately excelled him for inventiveness, and in his lifetime won an unchallenged position as the lock inventor without peer. His flair for naming his inventions did him no harm in the highly competitive bank lock industry. He had the Yale Infallible Bank Lock in 1851 or 1852, with a changeable key. He produced the Yale Magic Bank Lock, and modified that to create the Yale Double Treasury Bank Lock, which was perhaps the last great lock to operate solely by keys. When in about 1862 he fashioned the

Yale Monitor Bank Lock he was making the transition from the key lock to the dial or combination bank lock. The Yale Double Dial Bank Lock a year later may be said to have set basic standards for bank lock construction. Each dial controlled a stack of four circular tumblers, each tumbler could have one hundred changes, with a total number of possible combinations said to exceed one hundred million. Linus Yale, Jr., now spent years, until his death in 1868, in perfecting his Cylinder Lock for everyday security uses. It is, of course, through these locks with their small, flat keys that the Yale name achieved its international reputation.

The Yales were far from the only American lockmakers of stature. There were so many, one can only mention the most gifted, like James Sargent whose magnetic lock appeared in 1866, and who perfected the first model of a time lock in 1873, and Walter Schlage, the modern lock inventor.

Above: Day and Newell combination lock. When key turned, 83 different parts moved at once. Steel. Made about 1838. 9 x 12⅜ x 2 in.

Opposite: Holmes Electric Time Lock, operated by watch movements and electric batteries, for vaults. Steel. Patented 1872. 5⅛ x 9 x 3¼ in. John L. Mossman Collection of Locks and Keys, New York.

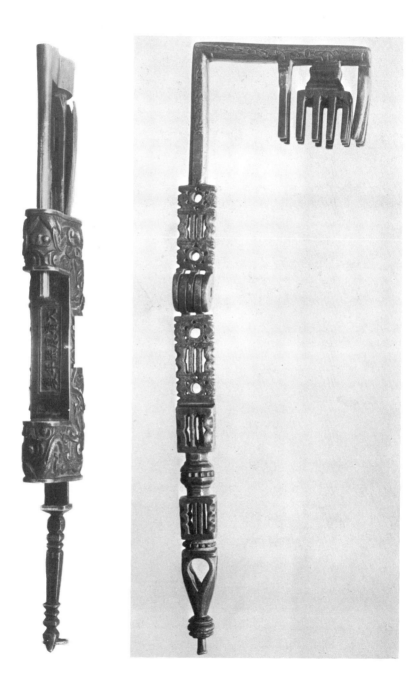

CHAPTER X

The Dating of Keys

"Turn the key deftly in the oiled wards
And seal the hushed Casket of My Soul."
                                        —John Keats

A WORD OF CAUTION on the dating of locks and keys: with such exceptions as a lock plate or a key inscribed with a date, all dates for locks and keys are approximate. If the name of the locksmith is inscribed, that, of course, makes it easier, for generally there is information on when the locksmith flourished. And, within the limits of style—Roman, Gothic, Renaissance, and so on—approximate dates can be reasonably accurate.

Occasionally, a key may be dated with almost precise accuracy. For example, the Visconti family of Milan celebrated a wedding with a member of the Savoy family in the Renaissance period. For the occasion a French locksmith was engaged and a handsome key was made for an elegant marriage coffret for the princely couple. We have that key. The shield of the Viscontis, with the wriggling serpent, is on one side, the shield of the Savoys, with its cross, on the other. Since we know that such a marriage was held in 1520, it is reasonable to date this charming key to that year; conceivably it could have been chiseled out the year before: 1519.

A similarly precise date is provided by the rare Persian mosque key of bronze on which the lower portion of the shank is inscribed with the name of Sultan Mohammad Khandabanda. We know that the Sultan reigned 1578–1587. On the bit is the name of the locksmith Riza ibn Ali and the Moslem date 988, that is, A.H. or After the Hegira, equivalent to our year 1580.

Next to such a definite date is the regnal dating. The Chinese, who from the Ming dynasties marked their beautiful porcelains with regnal dates, some-

Left: Chinese padlock, shown open, made for Emperor K'ang Hsi (1662-1722). Bronze. Closed: 5⅛ in.; open: 11½ in. Courtesy Frank Caro, New York. Right: Persian mosque swivel key, inscribed with name of Sultan Mohammad Khandabanda (1578–1587). Bronze. 12½ in. Museum of Fine Arts, Boston.

times also dated other objects of merit. A pair of identical bronze padlocks made for the Emperor K'ang Hsi, and carved with Imperial dragons, are cast with the six characters that give the *nien-hao,* or regnal dates 1662–1722. One of these, never published before, is shown (page 76). Later Chinese padlocks of brass are common; the dated locks of bronze are rare.

English locksmiths seem to have been the first to sign their locks. The royal locksmith Joseph Key, who created a number of magnificent locks for St. James's Palace and Hampton Court, the latter at a cost of eight hundred pounds, between 1700 and 1720, often inscribed his name on his works.

John Wilkes of Birmingham signed his "Johannes Wilkes de Birmingham fecit." Since he worked in the early eighteenth century we can fix approximate dates for his products. Wilkes made the large detector lock with the figure of a soldier in relief over the keyhole. That left leg, which is lifted so peculiarly, actually works on a rivet and when let down conceals the keyhole.

Another handsome lock bears the signature "Philip Harris Londoni fecit." Harris worked in London around 1700.

With such exceptions, dating depends upon educated judgments. No beginner should attempt it, but anyone who has studied—and has physically handled—numerous locks and keys may date by metal, style and workmanship. To call a key "Roman" is to indicate that it was made *somewhere* within the Roman empire, which can mean either Italy or any of the far-flung Roman domains from Iberia and Gaul to Egypt and Syria, from the second century B.C. to the third century A.D. Unless a lock or key is from a datable excavation —for example, from Pompeii or Herculaneum, which were wiped out in A.D. 79—any given date must be approximate. But Roman keys are not difficult to recognize.

Happily, Egyptian and Coptic keys are easy to identify. Once a few are seen, the styles are remembered. The Gothic key is another easily recognized. Keys of the transitional decades are not so easy to identify. Locksmiths did not stop suddenly to work in one style and begin in another. So there are keys in which the style of one era is still evident, with the "new" style discernibly creeping in.

Strong examples of craftsmanship, like the French Renaissance masterpiece keys, are never hard to place. However, many of this type were imitated in the nineteenth century to supply avid key collectors, and so caution is advised. Locks, more difficult to construct, were less often faked than keys.

Slowly, one learns to move among the periods and the styles. The "Chamberlain" keys, produced in the eighteenth century in England and in several European countries, are readily identified because they are usually of gilt brass rather than steel. These Chamberlain keys were not to be used in locks but were worn as badges of office or position and were pinned to silken rosettes. A novice, failing to note that they are of brass rather than of steel, can easily date them in an earlier century.

The ordinary museum, committed to "art," closes its locks and keys with the eighteenth century. Modern collectors, however, aware that they are assembling the specimens for which tomorrow's museums will have to find accommodation, are quietly gathering locks and keys from the early years of the Industrial Revolution. It is worth looking for a Barron or a Bramah or a Chubb or even an early Linus Yale, Sr. or Jr.—worth looking for and, it must be added, not easy to find.

As to dating, we are on firmer ground from the mid-nineteenth century. The later mechanisms were patented, and the date of the patent is our guide. For example, no cylinder lock can be dated earlier than 1857, the year when Linus Yale, Jr., patented his first cylinder lock.

Patent key lock by Linus Yale, Sr., one of first pin-tumbler locks. Steel. 5½ x 5¼ x 2½ in. John L. Mossman Collection of Locks and Keys, New York.

Yale Magic Bank Lock with changeable key, by Linus Yale, Jr. Steel. 9 x 9¼ x 2¼ in. John L. Mossman Collection of Locks and Keys, New York.

CHAPTER XI

Locks and Keys Tomorrow

"For thee I'll lock up all the gates of love."
—Much Ado About Nothing

WITH THE NEW INTEREST in design that came in at the end of the nineteenth century, architects and designers began to pay attention to the door as an organic part of any building. It was natural that the free spirit that soon dominated ornamentation should affect even so relatively small an object as the lock. After the cylinder and pin-tumbler advances, innovations in the construction of the lock were few, but its physical presentation began to profit from the emphasis on hardware styling.

When in 1920 Walter Schlage perfected his cylindrical locking mechanism and pioneered the push-button locking mechanism within the knob, attention could be concentrated on styling the lock and the knob in the new metals and in the decors acceptable to the multi-story skyscraper world. The cumbersome, the awkward, the slipshod in lockware could be forgotten. Escutcheons, lever handles and auxiliary locks all were redesigned afresh. Durability and quality could be guaranteed, while beauty of finish was there to be enjoyed.

Eaton, Yale & Towne commissioned fine contemporary artists to let their imaginations dream up door ornamentations in the modern temper. Many did, with escutcheons and door knobs, notably the brilliant Fernand Léger, Andrea Spadini, Isamu Noguchi, and also Jacques Lipschitz. The Italian Mirko made a lever handle that is like a bird form.

Slowly then, in the new renaissance that is taking place, the lock, which the Egyptians invented and which has so long served mankind, is being given a new wardrobe in bright, attractive and wholly modern forms. Tomorrow may suddenly bring radical and even more fetching designs.

The great craftsmen of the past, prior to the eighteenth century, leaned toward beauty rather than security. With the advent of Barron, Bramah and Chubb, and then Andrews, Newell and Day, the two Yales, Sargent and

Schlage, the emphasis swung to security. Now, thanks to splendid engineering which makes close tolerances possible in the machining of locks, plus the inspiration that is stimulating modern artists, we may expect before long a generation of locks and keys that will be fairer to the eye than even the ornate objets d'art traditionally cherished in the museums.

Above: American padlock. Brass. 19th century. Yale & Towne Lock Collection.

Opposite: "Grasshopper" lock made by the Herring Company. Steel. 1848. 14¾ x 11 x 2½ in. John L. Mossman Collection of Locks and Keys, New York.

Page 84: Replica of sickle-shaped Greek temple key. Original from Temple of Artemis, Lusoi, Arcadia. Ca. 700 B.C. Yale & Towne Lock Collection.

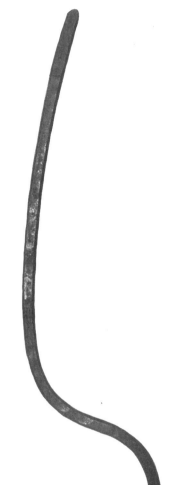

COURTNEY, CHARLES. *Unlocking Adventure,* in collaboration with Tom Johnson. Whittlesey House, New York, 1942.

CURRER-BRIGGS, NOEL. Editor, *Contemporary Observations on Security from Chubb Collectanea, 1818-1968.* Chubb and Son's Lock and Safe Company Limited, London, 1968.

ERAS, VINCENT J. M. *Locks and Keys Throughout the Ages.* N.p., Amsterdam, 1957.

FRANK, EDGAR B. *Old French Ironwork: The Craftsman and His Art.* Cambridge, 1950.

HOPKINS, ALBERT A. *The Lure of the Lock.* The General Society of Mechanics and Tradesmen, New York, 1928.

KAUFFMAN, HENRY J. *Early American Ironware: Cast and Wrought.* Charles E. Tuttle Company, Rutland, 1966.

MALLET, BART. *The Construction of Locks,* compiled from the papers of A. C. Hobbs, Esq., of New York and edited by Charles Tomlinson, Esq., London, 1868.

D'ALLEMAGNE, H. R. *Ferronerie Ancienne.* Catalog du Musée Le Secq des Tournelles, 2 vols., Paris, 1924.

DU MONCEAU, DUHAMEL. *Art du Serrurier.* Paris, 1767.

HOEVER, OTTO. *An Encyclopaedia of Ironwork: Examples of Hand Wrought Ironwork from the Middle Ages to the End of the 18th Century.* Berlin, n.d.

VIOLLET-LE-DUC. *Dictionnaire Raisonné du Mobilier Français de l'Epoque Carlovingienne à la Renaissance.* 6 vols., Paris, 1855.